Testimonials

"David Jaanz is a master of the art of ingenuity. He sees in artists what normal people don't see. He sees brilliance very early on in an artist's journey and he is able to cultivate talent like no other singing teacher or life coach in this country."

– Michael Parisi, Managing Director of Right Hand Management / Vinyl Tap Podcast

"David has always pushed his students to the best they can be and has elevated them to levels that are incredible due to attention to detail and an amazing approach to voice and music. He goes the extra yard in nurturing someone's voice and their simple wellbeing."

– Isaiah Firebrace, Winner of "The X Factor" Australia 2016

"I have worked with David Jaanz on multiple projects over several decades. David has an extraordinary gift for spotting talent at an early stage and an even greater gift for nurturing and encouraging these lucky people. He imbues confidence and ensures that his students achieve their potential and beyond."

– Graeme Rowland, Former Executive Producer of Seven Network

"Hard work works."

– Ralph Carr

"What the mind can envision you can achieve. Only one thing makes a champion: state of mind. Self-belief, passion, commitment, determination, discipline, obsession and the willingness to make sacrifices – this is all a state of mind. If you can see your vision, you will make it happen."

– Areti Anagnostellis, Four Times WFF Miss Figure Universe, World-Renowned Body Sculpting Coach

"David Jaanz personifies the relentless pursuit of excellence through a never ceasing, never fading energy fueled by the desire to inspire and encourage each person he meets to be the greatest version of themselves. Having impacted countless lives (including my own), David, in my opinion, will forever be one of the most unsung heroes of the Australian/global music industry."

– Jarrad Rogers, President of NOIZE Group Pty Ltd

"This is essential reading for all music students starting out in the real world. They will absolutely benefit from David's long-running experience in the world of music education and his extensive insight into the mindset required to succeed in the very challenging big wide world."

– Chong Lim AM, Composer, Music Producer and Musical Director of the Victorian State Schools Spectacular

"My dear friend David Jaanz is not just a singing teacher, but a beacon of guidance for young singers. His melodies of wisdom resonate deeply, teaching us that greatness is not forged in shortcuts but in unwavering dedication. With each turn of the page, he empowers us to shatter boundaries and reach new heights. To be guided by such an incredible man is to embark on a harmonious journey where dreams take flight, and the music within us finds its resounding voice. Thank you for everything you do for all young singers, David, and me included. I hope those reading this book will feel that guidance from you."

– Delta Goodrem, International
Recording Artist and Superstar

Champions Don't Do Cheat Days

Champions Don't Do Cheat Days

Secrets of the superachievers

DAVID JAANZ

A catalogue record for this book is available from the National Library of Australia

"Superachievers have a different mindset,
desire, passion level and work ethic to
most. They are driven by an inner hunger
and obsession for greatness. They are the
most highly disciplined individuals on the
planet and the words 'compromise' and
'cheat days' do not exist in their universe."

David Jaanz

Dedication

I WOULD LIKE TO dedicate this book firstly to the most beautiful human on the planet, my biggest supporter, the love of my life and the most positive person I have ever known, my beloved wife, Lynn Jaanz.

To our beautiful children: Miguel, Emilio, Mia, Michael, Sandra and Joanne, and our grandchildren, Jocelyn, Nathan, Christopher and Maddi.

To my brother, Andrew Fernandez, and my parents, Dawn and Joe Fernandez, who never gave up on me and taught me to "Think Big".

Finally, I would like to thank my Lord and Saviour, Jesus Christ, who has never left me, and the Holy Spirit who makes every victory possible.

Contents

Introduction 1

Chapter One

Self-belief Is the Catalyst to Greatness 3

Chapter Two

The Power of the Alternate Mirror 19

Chapter Three

Build Your Brand 25

Chapter Four

Champions Don't Do Cheat Days 31

Chapter Five

Without Risk There Is No Greatness 41

Chapter Six

Find Your Superpower 49

Chapter Seven

Practise Extraordinary When Everyone
Is Practising Ordinary 59

Chapter Eight

Invest in Great Mentors 69

Chapter Nine

Goals Are Your Gold   73

Chapter Ten

Victory Starts with the Mouth   77

Chapter Eleven

Never Quit   81

Chapter Twelve

Put God First   85

Introduction

I NEVER FELT READY to write a book about success until now. We are always learning and growing, and although I have experienced huge success and victories in my youth, I feel there is something beautiful about age. Age brings wisdom and maturity. As the book of Ecclesiastes in the Bible says, "for everything there is a season", "a right time". I feel now is the time.

Champions Don't Do Cheat Days: Secrets of the Superachievers is a book filled with major keys to winning in life. I have coached thousands of singers over the years, national champions and Eurovision entrants. I am also a world champion myself, having represented Australia and winning the 1989 Nescafé and Yamaha Band Explosion World Championship, with my band Janz. So I am no stranger to winning and winning ways. I have also been blessed to have had some of the most extraordinary mentors in my life and have read hundreds of books on success over the years. I have been a student of success since I was 14 years old and was handed my first motivational tape series in the 1970s by my uncle

Dexter McKinnon, which totally transformed my way of thinking and outlook on life. Please enjoy my book and I pray you are changed and empowered to live a life of total victory.

ONE

Self-belief Is the Catalyst to Greatness

IT DOESN'T TAKE LONG to realise we live in a negative world. Many realise this very early in life, perhaps after our first encounter with bullying at the school playground or with some opinionated negative family members at family gatherings. I was a young coloured boy growing up in the UK in the 1960s when racism was rampant, and sadly this had a great impact on me. I was never invited to birthday parties, and no one came to mine. Other children would often bully me. This hurt greatly when, as a 5- or 6-year-old, you couldn't understand what you had done wrong or how the world works.

It took many years to heal the damage of my childhood as my self-belief took a huge blow and I felt unloved and excluded, like a leper. This set me on a path of always trying to seek the approval and validation of other people. Deep inside it was very hard to shake off the intense feeling of being worthless.

Sadly, a great number of us feel the same way in society today. Many people in this world are hurting and for various reasons have lost their hope, self-belief and ability to dream.

Eventually, as time went on, I was able to heal from this, as I explain later in my book.

The invisible enemy

The media is always pushing the doomsday stories of bad news happening in the world and, unfortunately, we are rarely told of any good news. We are flooded with reports about murders, crimes, how poorly the economy is doing, about the next pandemic, about how the world is heading for an inevitable cliff and a fall. We are told about wars, climate issues, rising interest rates, inflation, famines, and are constantly reminded that the future is looking bleak.

As a result of this constant bombardment of bad news many people simply can't help but be negative and pessimistic.

Consequently, the people around us, whether family members, school teachers or peers, can become disillusioned and develop a negative mindset and outlook on life, projecting and reinforcing this when they interact with us.

This can be in the form of negative words, body language and high degrees of pessimism hurled at us constantly, or negative encounters that can damage us in profound ways, stealing our dreams, dashing our hopes and stripping us of all self-belief.

Every great victory or conquest starts with self-belief. When self-belief is eroded or simply taken away, it is very hard to achieve anything great. It is a form of paralysis or blindness. This can be temporary, but often it becomes a permanent disability where we lose our ability to dream and to hope, and life becomes meaningless and pointless.

> Every great victory or conquest starts with self-belief.

"Without a vision, man perishes."

Proverbs 29:18 NKJ

This may be one of the tragic reasons for the increase in the reported suicide rates and depression among young people and in the general population. Take away a person's hope and they are left empty, with no reason to live.

Sadly, we are conditioned and trained by the media and society how to think and this plays out in our decisions and actions in our everyday lives.

The media and society work together to form what I call a type of "world system" that shapes and directs our every action and thought process.

This hypnotic type of effect is bolstered daily as we spend more and more time glued to social media sites, watching TV and socialising with other highly influential individuals who simply reinforce the universal pessimistic news, views and narrative.

Just look around at cafes, family gatherings, trams and trains – people are glued to their cell phones, obsessed with social media. There is very little real social interaction as social media has become a compulsion.

Our self-esteem is measured by the number of views and likes on our posts. We are graded by the masses and we're frequently willing to sell out on our core beliefs and values to get more likes or views on social media. Without realising it, we become "world system" slaves and addicts. Our self-worth, who we are, is solely based on the opinions of others.

Our obsession with self is deeply rooted in years of negativity and rejection. Deep inside there is an intense need to be loved and accepted, which is an intrinsic need of every human being.

The danger in our constant desire for acceptance of the masses is that we can lose ourselves in this shallow pursuit. In the process we may sell out by sacrificing our voice, freedom of expression, ideology, our authenticity and uniqueness.

> Deep inside there is an intense need to be loved and accepted, which is an intrinsic need of every human being.

We give in to conformity and just fit in with the masses, sacrificing our individuality in the pursuit of love and acceptance.

Many of the movie stars and celebrities in the world who find the acceptance of the masses still seem to live empty, unfulfilled lives. Some take their own lives or succumb to drug overdoses and other vices.

The invisible enemy is the prevailing world system which is often highly negative and causes immense damage to the human spirit, leading many people to breaking points as they struggle to fit in, be accepted and be loved.

The battle then is for restoration and healing of the damage inflicted by years of unconscious self-hate and rejection.

This is the fight to dream again, to think freely for the first time and to break the chains of limited thinking.

> *"If you know the enemy and know yourself, you need not fear the result of a hundred battles."*
>
> Sun Tzu, The Art of War

After working with thousands of students over the years, my belief is that every human being is endowed with the seeds of greatness and has unlimited potential. It all starts with restoring self-belief and then learning to develop a positive mental attitude and mindset.

As we break free from the programming and thinking of the world system, we start creating a new story for our lives, a new destiny. We start thinking for ourselves often for the first time and start creating the life we have always longed for with faith, new optimism and a renewed hope. Dreams suddenly become possibilities.

The heart

My belief is the heart is the most wonderful gift from God. Yes, it keeps us alive, but I have always believed that the treasures of our life are in our heart – our gifts, our talents, our greatness and, of course, our feelings and emotions.

"As a man thinketh in his heart, so is he."

Proverbs 23:7

It is almost like our hearts are under attack. When we continually experience negativity or feelings of never being good enough, we start to shut down. It is almost like we hear a voice in the atmosphere calling out "loser" and "never good enough". Even when no one is around, we hear this voice. It is like our subconscious constantly reminds us of our smallness and inadequacies.

> When we continually experience negativity or feelings of never being good enough, we start to shut down.

Over time we close off our hearts gradually, mask and guard our hearts. This is evident as we slowly lose our smiles, don't project or mumble when we talk, become shy and withdrawn and lose the energy and bounce we had when we were children. We seek and are driven to conformity, fitting in at any cost, and are just going through the daily motions of doing what's expected of us.

Over time, with a continual exposure to negativity from every angle, we are programmed to think defeat, think we are just nothing special and close off our hearts more and more.

I am not a doctor, but I have often thought sickness and disease are caused by this shutting down of our hearts, eroding of our confidence, losing the child-like spark and energy, losing our smiles and joy. Perhaps sickness manifests because people have a sick heart. A sick heart is perhaps caused by this shutdown. Perhaps health will be restored, as self-belief and faith in one's self is restored, when we start to dream again, find and fulfil the purpose of our lives. At least this may be part of it all.

> As a coach and mentor, I have always known the journey to greatness is an inner one.

As a coach and mentor, I have always known the journey to greatness is an inner one, a journey of inner healing, restoration and growth, and as you heal with the inner and deepest part of your being, the outer greatness manifests and is released.

Restoring self-belief

I believe we were born to be loved, to seek love and to be loving. I believe we are made in the image of God, and God is love. We are from God, and therefore our capacity to love and be loved is in our nature.

I truly believe the greatest disease in the world is lack of self-belief. It causes people to not fulfil their true potential, not use their gifts, not recognise their strengths and, therefore, not realise their true life potential. We are given gifts as a key to unlock our destiny. I will discuss this in a later chapter.

Here are some keys to restoring your self-belief, healing a damaged heart and unmasking.

1. **Do affirmations daily.** There is a beautiful scripture I love and it says, "There is life and death in the power of the tongue" (Proverbs 18:21). Repeated affirmations are powerful. Some affirmations that I recommend are:

   - I have greatness in me.
   - I have a restored, healed heart.
   - I am a champion.
   - I am fearfully and wonderfully made.
   - I am destined to reign.
   - My uniqueness is my power.

- I have the right to my own free thinking and ideas.
- I am no longer a slave to the world system.

Please feel free to write down your own affirmations.

Kurt Lewin, a German American psychologist, once said, "An individual's behaviour is a function of the person, including their history, personality and motivation, and their environment."

We are basically the words that have been spoken to us, and the experiences that we have had. As we practise changing our words, and carefully guarding our mouths and watching the words we say, we can dramatically change the trajectory of our lives.

2. **Be careful who your friends are.** You cannot afford the luxury of negative people in your life. Find friends who encourage and lift you up. Negativity is like a big anchor pulling you down and steering you away from your dreams and victory.

3. **Become a student of success.** Read as many books on success as you can. Watch inspirational videos.

4. **Find some form of spirituality or ideology that works for you.** Faith gives you a counter-narrative, an alternate mirror to see yourself in. Over time, with a strong faith, you replace the mirror of the world system with a mirror of a higher consciousness.

> Faith gives you a counter-narrative, an alternate mirror to see yourself in.

5. **Start a "thankful" journal about the things you are thankful for.** Often we tend to focus on all the negatives in life. Wisdom comes when we realise bad things happen to good people. This is part of life – we get hurt, discouraged, tough stuff happens ... The key is finding the inner strength to get up and keep moving. Just keep moving.

6. **Find mentors who encourage and believe in you.** Great mentors are priceless.

So, start believing in you. Yes, YOU.

When we swap the mirror of the world system to the mirror of a higher consciousness, we realise the way we see ourselves is all "programming" and "conditioning".

In summary, we create and control our own reality and destiny when we choose the words spoken to us that we may accept or reject.

Discovering the superstar in you

"You are fearfully and wonderfully made, made in the image of God. You are invincible, unstoppable, unbeatable in him."

Psalm 139:14

Interestingly, in the movies and comic books, Superman always wears thick glasses and a big suit as a disguise to mask his true identity. Underneath his clothes, he is the man of steel, "superman". Similarly, non-fictitious human beings also wear masks. These masks are also real – invisible, but real.

The mask we wear may be created by negative thinking, lack of self-belief, insecurity, worry, conformity, other people's opinions and fear. We can't see it, but it's real. Everybody wears a mask of some form to survive in the jungle called life. The mask is a defence mechanism to stop ourselves from getting hurt, so we hide, pretend and create an invisible but real veneer so no one sees our true identity.

As we heal over time, and revelation comes, we slowly start removing these masks and the real us emerges: your superhero, genius or superstar.

In the field of body building, there is a diet phase where the body builder starts getting leaner in preparation for a competition. As the athlete gets closer to competing, they go on a strict diet phase which is the hardest of all phases. As the excess weight and body fat is removed, the definition of the body builder is revealed. Underneath you see the true body definition and toning.

> We hide, pretend and create an invisible but real veneer so no one sees our true identity.

We wear different masks in different situations – with our family, one mask; friends, another mask. This is evident in our behaviour in different circumstances, and the way we talk and communicate changes with different people.

Often we wear these masks to conform or fit in. With many people, we are discouraged from having an unpopular opinion or from expressing our truth or true personality. This is evident in the heavy censorship of social media, and the selective reporting of mainstream media. We are treated like sheep – just fed a narrative, censored so we can't think, and the majority of people are so hypnotised they become agents of this conformity machine to reinforce the narrative. We have forgotten how to research and think outside the box. We only obey and accept the mainstream narratives.

Sadly, this describes most people. This is the majority mask and what I call the conformed mask.

> We have forgotten how to research and think outside the box.

Over time, we lose ourselves, we lose our identities and just mask permanently. We join the sheep. We eat the same standard food, have the same habits, talk the same way and become the same. Before we know it, we are immersed in average, and just blend in with the masses. Sometimes even our language and what we adorn our bodies with is an inner yearning to fit in.

On the flip side, when we unmask, we may choose a unique style as a brand statement. We are conscious, our uniqueness is our power, and we are brand builders (branding discussed later). Our true potential can only be revealed when we are brave enough, restored and healed enough to unmask to find our true identity and reveal ourselves.

Unmasking, and realising your true potential, often takes years of healing, wisdom, enlightenment and revelation.

It also may require some time away from what some may call the "rat race" of life and finding a space and time to think, reflect and contemplate.

This helps us stop, take a long breath and hit the reset button as we assess where we want to go next in our lives.

TWO

The Power of the Alternate Mirror

AS MENTIONED EARLIER, MOST of us validate or evaluate ourselves based on the mirror of the world system – other people's opinions, social media likes, status symbols, popularity – and for many this works.

However, there is an incredible freedom and feeling of liberation when we look for alternative sources of validation or alternate mirrors.

We feel the shackles and chains of expectation just drop off us – the stress leaves us, depression leaves and it is almost like we can "breathe" again.

There is a freedom when we don't need the approval of others and don't really care anymore what people think.

We run our own race, love our own lives, and build a life of significance based on a higher standard – our own standards, a different mirror.

We may also find we get healthier as our heart heals from the damaging effects of conformity, conditioning and hopelessness. We no longer hear the silent airwaves calling out "you are just a loser, not good enough, never good enough" as mentioned in Chapter 1.

Unfortunately, many remain in a state of constant discouragement and disillusionment as they struggle to gain acceptance and love in a system that can often reject us. Sometimes we feel that no matter how much fame, success or popularity we have, it is just never enough. We keep chasing this carrot called validation, true success and fulfilment that we can never quite catch or enjoy.

We are reminded of the celebrities and stars who have had tragic lives, many taking their own lives or caught in a web of substance abuse. It is like the mountain top called fame is not everything they expected or hoped for.

When we can leave or detach from the world mirror and create an alternate mirror, we see ourselves differently.

My firm belief is everyone should find an alternate mirror based on their own standards, beliefs and values.

People of all faiths and belief systems should seek to find or build their own mirrors, their own alternate validation measure or yardstick.

As a follower of Jesus, Christ is my mirror. The word is full of beautiful truths and by faith I believe these.

This is my mirror:

> *"I am fearfully and wonderfully made."*
>
> Psalm 139:14

> *"I have the abundance of Grace and gift of righteousness and am destined to reign."*
>
> Romans 5:17

> *"There is a plan for my life."*
>
> Jeremiah 29:11

> *"I am more than a conqueror."*
>
> Romans 8:31–39

There are so many more.

> My firm belief is everyone should find an alternate mirror.

This is my mirror and to me the "word" of God is greater than anything man or the world can say. This is my alternate mirror. What is your alternate mirror?

As we look into our alternate mirror, and start becoming students of success, we start changing the way we see ourselves.

This in essence is the law of attraction summarised, "As we start seeing victory in our minds we change the whole trajectory of our lives from attracting loss to attracting wins."

You have to start seeing and expecting success in your mind and heart.

Every victory starts with the mirror in which we see ourselves.

On a personal note, which you can take or leave – I also believe the holy word or word of God can go beyond changing your mirror and actually go deep and transform and heal the depths of your being and heart – reverse the damage of the war zone and put every cell and molecule in your body on a trajectory of victory, health and wellbeing. Most people are like rockets waiting to be launched ... Some have it all, but are never launched. They never light the rocket. The fire that lights this rocket is faith – yes, faith. Faith in yourself, faith in your dreams and, if you choose, faith in God.

*"Faith is the substance of things hoped,
for the evidence of things not seen."*

Hebrews 11:1

Start seeking or creating your own alternate mirror.

Imagine if every cell in your body and your mind was full of self-belief, and you truly believed "all things are possible". I believe people sabotage or destroy their destinies, through poor choices, speaking and thinking negatively, lack of self-belief, never taking off masks, limited vision and giving up on their dreams. I believe every cell in the human body comes alive when we allow ourselves to dream and to pursue a great endeavour or goal.

The greatest change you can make in your life is to find your alternate mirror.

The alternate mirror allows you to heal, restore, discover your own strengths and gifts and reignite your self-belief.

Your next step is when you have done the work on yourself don't be afraid to chase your dreams harder than before.

The alternate mirror allows you to run your own race, express your authentic you, your uniqueness, and deal with the ups and downs in life in a more positive way. You are confident, know your values and are sure of who you are, and are prepared to take the hits of life and bounce back.

There is more satisfaction when you no longer worry about getting your validation from the world system, and your self-worth comes from your validation point and your alternate mirror.

You take your alternate mirror into the world system, run your own race, avoid damage to your mind, body and spirit, and set and chase your own goals.

THREE

Build Your Brand

SUCCESSFUL PEOPLE, IN ALL walks of life, have a strong "personal brand". They lead the way with fresh ideas, distinctive appearance and have an energy and persona that makes them stand out from the crowd. They also use their gifts, talents and strengths to propel themselves to success and victory in their chosen fields. They understand that "uniqueness is power" and very deliberately choose to differentiate themselves and build their personal brand.

In the music industry, it's all about "point of difference" – having a unique tone, look, style, energy, image or vibe. It's then about building social media, advertising platforms and hit songs around this. The record label then pushes this unique brand and invests heavily in its success.

Similarly, in the world of business and products, marketing and product managers are always looking for the "point or points of difference" or areas where their products stand out and have the edge. They also then invest millions in advertising campaigns, social media and various promotions to push the product. They develop unique colours and a distinctive look for the product.

The pursuit of USPs (unique selling propositions) and branding often takes millions of dollars before the brand is even launched. Research, development and market testing takes months and years before a product even hits the market.

> Your work ethic needs to be on a whole other level. You cannot do average and expect to win.

Elite musicians often write 100–200 songs, pick the best 10 songs for the album, and then look for the "right producer". They invest in image, social media and branding strategists to help them stand out. The label then spends millions to launch the artist. This is why it is so hard to get a record or publishing deal. Your work ethic needs to be on a whole other level. You cannot do average and expect to win. Your dedication and commitment have to be at an elite level.

There are several business people who understand the concept of "personal branding". Richard Branson comes to mind. He has his own style of fashion and is very conscious and strategic about how he is perceived in the public. Football superstar Cristiano Ronaldo is the same – very stylish, very strategic and very specific in how he positions his public profile. There are many other names that are heavy marketers and build multi-million dollar empires simply because they are "brand conscious".

The journey to success, in business and in life, also starts with us understanding that we are like products and we are always "selling", whether we are aware of it or not, and whether we like it or not. The fact is, we are in a world of people and people are greatly influenced and hypnotised by social media, TV, music, magazines, celebrities and peers, as discussed in earlier chapters.

As mentioned, time and time again people are heavily programmed and influenced, and this affects and conditions people's perceptions.

When we understand this principle, we start seeing the importance of building our own personal brand.

To build your own personal brand you need to understand your personality, gifts and talents. Look for the areas that you shine in, you flow in, and let this be part of the build.

A great smile, bubbly personality and great sense of humour can be part of your brand. Similarly, being quiet, serious and conservative could be part of your brand.

> Every human is different, so do not be afraid to be different and magnify the difference.

Every human is different, so do not be afraid to be different and magnify the difference.

Don't be afraid to "fit out" – let your brand be bold. BE BOLDLY YOU.

Next, look at your imaging and be conscious of your styling. Try to be as authentic as possible and remember a personal brand does not have to be like anyone – it can be subtle and yet strong.

I have always believed "uniqueness is power", so build the unique you.

Building your personal brand is often a slow process, as we have been so conditioned to fit in – think the same, act the same and look the same. It starts with unmasking, which may take several years or decades.

Sadly, most people never unmask, and spend their lives only in the land of conformity and wanting to be like someone else.

It is almost like we need to come out of this box we are put in by conformity, peer pressure and society, or we build "conformity brands" not true "unique personal brands".

As you start looking into alternate mirrors and building your self-belief, the "lion" in you emerges, your genius awakens and the giant in you arises.

The "new you" or "real you" will start the process of thinking for yourself and having your own ideas and beliefs.

It is the transformation from within that manifests in the transformation on the outer.

This is the foundation of every great brand – a high degree of self-awareness.

Start being conscious of your personal brand, start building it and don't be afraid to stand out from the crowd.

One of the great secrets of success is that the greatest leaders and influencers have consciously, accidentally or through natural growth and evolution built strong personal brands.

Elvis Presley was criticised for the way he looked, moved and sang; the Beatles were criticised for their haircuts. Today, there is a whole generation of Elvis impersonators,

> Start being conscious of your personal brand, start building it and don't be afraid to stand out from the crowd.

and the Beatles still influence so, so many global artists.

The choice is yours: blend in or build a powerful personal brand!

Brand builders are not sheep. They are leaders who have their own style, look, opinions and vision. They know that uniqueness is power, innovation is king and their originality is their currency. They unmask, build their own life and run their own race. They are highly motivated and committed to greatness. Brand builders lead the way with new ideas, innovation and ingenuity.

FOUR

Champions Don't Do Cheat Days

IT IS NOT EASY to be a champion.

It is not easy to be an elite athlete, swimmer or anyone who is a high achiever. It takes extreme commitment to winning, extreme commitment to your dreams and goals, overcoming heartbreak, obstacles, defeat and rejection. It takes a fierce determination to break the mould of normal that we are propelled towards and conditioned to settle for.

It is not easy being a champion or winning. You have to have an obsession for greatness! So, you will find most superachievers do not do cheat days and are high disciplinarians.

The term "cheat day", according to the Oxford Dictionary, refers to "a day on which a person following a diet disregards restrictions on the amount or kinds of food they can eat."

It was created to promote a compromise within strict, unachievable diets. The problem with this is that is it **NOT consistent**.

> Some people can do cheat days and manage to bounce back, however, the majority of us lose momentum towards our goals.

Some people can do cheat days and manage to bounce back, however, the majority of us lose momentum towards our goals, and the break in routine can be damaging. The break in routine is often catastrophic and this break in routine is why so many set a goal and then quit.

Compromise is the Killer of Dreams

The problem with cheat days is that ONE day can quickly become EVERY day.

Compromise becomes the norm, habit and lifestyle. Once a habit is formed, it is hard to shake or change.

This is most people today. They compromise their way through life.

They blame God, other people, life and circumstances, but never take ownership of the fact that the lack of total commitment to their goals and dreams has caused the demise of their dreams or unfulfilled lives.

Taking stock of my life, I have also fallen victim of compromise and cheat days. Yes, I have been tremendously successful in my life, but there is always another level and greater heights I could have gone to if I only applied myself more and not fallen victim of the break in routine. I have failed at hundreds of diets because of compromise, paid full year subscriptions at gyms that I have not gone to, had songs I never finished and goals and dreams left unfinished and incomplete.

This is the disastrous effect of "cheat days" – you break your flow, your rhythm, and it is hard to get back in the groove.

The good news is that new positive habits can be formed with dedication and consistency. Just keep doing it every day and eliminate compromise.

The Bible talks about counting the cost of "building a house". We need to know the cost of dreams before we embark on them – sacrifice, financial investment, resilience, discipline and character.

I always say to my students that you can have the greatest voice in the world but if you don't develop the mindset and work ethic of champions, you most likely won't succeed.

Bad habits catch up with you, and compromise catches up with you. It's the smallest details that can result in the millisecond win for an athlete, or making the rugby/soccer team, or winning a competition.

> Bad habits catch up with you and compromise catches up with you.

In my experience observing young stars, many stop lessons when they have some small degree of success. This is their biggest mistake, as they change routine and cease doing the little things that got them there, including weekly mentoring and lessons. Mentors keep you accountable, and the higher you go on the success ladder, the more you need to lean in, work harder and refine your talent. These artists often struggle, and success almost stops as their busyness, or perhaps pride to a degree, takes over and they don't understand why it's not working out. My advice, "Go back to when you were winning, and do the things that got you there!"

Keep doing what you were doing in the beginning to get you there, but do it with more intensity and purpose. Stay at lessons, honour your mentors, stay at the gym, don't change your diet and keep your close friends who loved and supported you – this is gold.

Everyone should be a student of success. Sadly, this is not part of the curriculum in schools. We teach our young people many subjects, but "how to win in life" is not generally taught as part of the greater curriculum.

I hope this book sits by your bedside table for life, and you refer to it often. There are many other wonderful books and tutorials on success. Invest your time in being a student of winning and success.

It is not easy to be a champion.

Champions speak differently, think differently and may have to eat differently. They go to bed at certain times. They are highly organised and efficient planners.

My wife and I are vegans who don't use oil when cooking. We follow the Dr McDougall Starch Solution protocol. When we are out socially, this makes our options very limited, so we have to say "no" a lot, or advise family members and friends of our dietary requirements before going out. We refuse to compromise, and we follow this principle preached in this chapter. For many years, I struggled with my weight until I found the Starch Solution and Dr McDougall (www.drmcdougall.com).

Don't be afraid to be the odd one. Sometimes you need to "stand out" rather than "fit in" to find greatness.

As a young singer, I was always practising my vocal exercises two or three times a day, was always at lessons two to three times a week with my voice coaches, wrote songs seven days a week, learnt keyboard and composition. I never stopped dreaming about making it big. I would pretend to sign autographs, put up goals on my cupboard door, and maintained a high degree of discipline and excellence.

I truly believe I outworked most of my peers in the industry at the time and ended up becoming a world champion with my band Janz, winning the World Yamaha Band Competition in 1989.

In fact, we were possibly the hardest working band in Australia in the late 1980s, early '90s.

In any given field the superachievers hold this secret close to their hearts.

What song have you been given?

In the world of reality TV singing competitions, singers often don't get to choose the song they will be performing at key moments in the show.

Songs are usually preselected, then given to the singers to perform at the various stages of the competition.

In so many cases, the songs do not suit the singer, may not be in the singer's style, and I have even seen songs chosen in the wrong key for the contestant.

Many singers look at these TV shows for validation of their artistry, even with this immense possibility of poor song selection, in addition to the politics and behind-the-scene games of television.

Most singers go in blind to this fact, and viewers have no idea. The machine then clicks in, and the general public think the best singer is chosen, only to see that most of the winners vanish and no one knows where they are months or years later when the singles that are written for them flop and fail to get radio or commercial air play.

> Often the artist most likely to succeed is knocked out in the earlier rounds, or not even chosen for the show.

Often the artist most likely to succeed is knocked out in the earlier rounds, or not even chosen for the show.

This is because the "real world" of the music industry is based on unique artists who write innovative music, and not necessarily those who can belt the highest note and copy another singer.

Although my students have won all these competitions, with several runners-up, over the years, my emphasis is always building the "unique artist" and encouraging all my students to learn an instrument and start songwriting.

Emotion Centred Singing, our teaching approach at Jaanz International Singing Academy, has always been "the evolution of the singer into the artist".

The wrong song is the cruellest blow to a promising artist. They may have trained for many years and may have original songs that cannot be showcased on a cover-only TV show, but may end up giving up on their dreams after the "wrong song" or not doing well in the competition.

In life, we may be given the "wrong song" in a sense. The wrong song is negative feedback from peers, mentors, family members and often our own mind and negative self-talk. We may be born into a negative family, lived under abusive conditions, or may have been bullied and ostracised at school. These can be viewed as "wrong song" situations.

We carry these "wrong songs" throughout our lives, and often receive them from people who have done nothing successful – no track record of wins, many are naturally critical or have failed in life or are perhaps frustrated at an unfulfilled life. Sadly, some of these people have inflicted abuse or bullying on us.

Everyone has an opinion and always remember it's an opinion but may not be the truth. You often find the people often most unqualified in a particular field usually have the most opinions. We often take these opinions to heart and many abort their dreams as a result of these opinions.

My advice is to only take opinions from those with a track record of success or who have been up the mountain top of success.

In my life I have learnt to dismiss opinions from those unqualified to advise me. I have always learnt the principle of "flying with eagles".

"Eagles" are those I consider champions and successes in their respective fields.

I consciously seek out the best, those with a track records of success, and seek their advice and counsel on important issues.

The tragedy about social media comments is these comments are just opinions, many are negative and can be damaging and dream stealers.

In the earlier chapters I discussed how the majority of people are programmed to be "negative" by the world system.

Therefore, it makes sense that there may be a majority of negative, derogatory comments on some of our social media posts. Ignore these and keep moving forward. Don't let these comments steal your determination and drive to chase your dreams.

Artists and entrepreneurs use the power of social media to build their brand, so delete or ignore the negativity, keep going for the win and build your fan base.

The good news is, no matter what cards life has handed you, you can bounce back – you can win! Examine your life today and see whether you have been a victim of the "wrong song".

The wrong song is not who you are!

Always remember that an opinion is not a fact. Don't let anybody steal your vision and dream.

FIVE

Without Risk There Is No Greatness

"Walk by faith and not by sight."

2 Corinthians 5:7

I HAD DONE HUNDREDS of singing lessons, performed as a singer at several shows, had finished a bachelor's degree in business, and was cruising as an export marketing executive at an international company. The money was great, I travelled in business class all around the world and was on a fast track to the top in the corporate world.

In the middle of this, I was burning the candle at both ends trying to be a high-flying corporate star during the day and a singing star at night and on the weekend. I had shows and gigs until late at night, then would get up early for work in the morning, followed by after-work rehearsals with my band, as well as squeezing in time for singing lessons, my own practice and time with family and friends. I eventually paid a heavy price for this, as I found myself in the ICU after falling asleep at the wheel driving home at 2 am after a show.

> To this day, no one knows who pulled me out of my car, which was a write-off, and the doctors do not know how I survived.

To this day, no one knows who pulled me out of my car, which was a write-off, and the doctors do not know how I survived. All of my ribs were cracked, my lung collapsed, and I have scars on my body to remind me every day that I was given a second chance and this was my miracle! When life gets tough, I just look at the giant scar in the middle of my chest where the doctors opened me up to save me, and I keep the faith, keep fighting and keep believing in a higher plan. Whether we are victims of abuse, broken families, tears, broken hearts, or missed opportunities, all of this results in a visible scar, or a scar in our hearts of some sort. Rather than avoiding the scars, trust that the scars make us like warriors, fighters in this war zone called life. We need to look at these scars and remind ourselves to keep pushing on. We are not where we were, and scars, setbacks and defeats can be the substance of greatness.

Often our scars become the reason why we want to succeed in life. They become the reason we fight to overcome and to win. The key is not staying down from life's hits, but getting up and fighting another day.

Our scars should propel us to be stars in life.

Up to this point, my life was great, but I was thoroughly exhausted every day and every night. While performing at a bar one night, legendary manager Ralph Carr saw me and started mentoring me. One day he said to me, "I think you've got what it takes to make it. Leave your day job. Leave the band you are in right now. I want you to work with Robert Parde (a brilliant keyboard player and writer). I want you to write as a full-time job, Monday to Friday, 9 to 5. I want you to train harder and I also want you to slowly recruit band members for your new band. I want you to lose weight, get fit and grow your hair, take singing lessons, keyboard lessons ... work."

At the time, I didn't realise that Ralph was building my brand, giving me a fast-track course on how to win, and teaching me that without risk, there is no greatness. The first thing I felt when Ralph said this was fear. What would my Indian family think? How could I leave an amazing job? How could I leave my security?!

After weeks of contemplation, and my mum's reluctant blessing, I found the courage to risk it all, roll the dice of life and go for my dreams, do what I loved doing most and pursue my strongest gift – singing!

One of the keys to helping me make my decision was lying in hospital at the point of death, in the ICU after the car accident. Lying there struggling to breathe, with tubes down my throat, wondering if I would ever be able to sing again, I made the decision in my heart that my life could have ended that night in my car alone and without any help. I also made the decision to never be afraid of risk, as we never know when we will take our last breath.

The rest is history. Two years after leaving my day job, my band Janz won the 1989 Nescafé and Yamaha Band Explosion World Championship, beating 22,000 bands from around the world and representing Australia. We were signed to Sony music and released a few great singles. I then went on to have several successful years as a professional singer performing regularly on television and at Grand Hyatt Melbourne, and have since gone on to become one of the most successful singing coaches and star makers on the planet, with hundreds of successful students locally and internationally. I am the only coach in the world whose students have won all of the major TV competitions, and several have been runners-up.

My firm belief is that life is short – too short. Don't be afraid to listen to your heart, take calculated risks and go for what is in your heart. Go for your dreams. If I hadn't taken the risk, I wouldn't be living the dream, and yes, I am living the dream, and later I will talk about this.

Yes, there were setbacks and at times fear came back in and I felt like going back to the safety net of security … trying to find a day job. I am so happy I did not retreat.

Ralph Carr had, and still has, a great influence on my life. He has gone on to be one of the greatest managers on the planet, building many superstar acts, and now is heavily involved in sports management. Ralph is still a mentor and close friend whom I love dearly. Without him, I would probably still be in a 9–5 job and would have never had the courage to build the most amazing life. He is the mentor of mentors, and the one who gave me the courage to take risks and go for gold.

Without risk there is no greatness.

There will be times when no one will see your dream. You can't explain your dream to others because it is a little voice in your heart telling you this is what you should be doing right now. Often it will not make sense

> Don't be afraid to listen to your heart, take calculated risks and go for what is in your heart. Go for your dreams.

to those around you. That little voice has caused many great people to rise and perform incredible exploits. Study the greats, the history makers, and you will find they listened, obeyed and won.

Arguably the greatest soccer player in the world, Cristiano Ronaldo, left his home in Portugal at the age of 12, to train at a pro club and stayed in dormitories away from his family. They would find him running on treadmills with weights on his legs at 12 years old, training late at night when his peers were asleep so he could be better and faster. Later in life, when soft drink bottles were put in front of him at a press conference, he instinctively removed them and replaced them with water. That to me said it all. Yes, champions operate on a different level, risk everything and don't do cheat days.

Great people see dreams or goals by "faith first and not by sight". This means, they see with the eyes of the heart, in the invisible. When we practise seeing dreams in the invisible as often as possible, it can manifest in the natural or reality.

Dream it, then action it with doing the right things. Cristiano saw himself as the best soccer player in the world, and then trained and committed to his goals with an incredible routine and discipline. Every night, when he was 12 years old on the treadmill, I am sure he would see himself as the best player in the world – I think he is the best of all time.

"Faith without works is dead."
James 2:14 NKJ

So, yes, see your dream and then work for it. Plan for it. (Note, there is also a whole spiritual aspect to this scripture that I will not break down. I am using it in relation to dreams.)

Let your dream become a magnificent obsession.

The greatest boxer of all time, Muhammad Ali, would wake up early in the morning at 4 or 5 am and start training. He would start with a run, then hit the gym, then do boxing training etc. The training regime for swimmers is also intense, with early morning rises and training for hours, often seven days a week, and matched by a much regulated diet. The key is a very strict timetable, discipline and organisation.

> Let your dream become a magnificent obsession.

Similarly, the highest achievers I know treat life the same way and have an athlete's mentality and training regime in their business and life. The key is committing to a dream, and then getting excited enough and committed enough to wake up and do the work. Let your dream become a magnificent obsession.

When your dream becomes a magnificent obsession, you want to get up early, you want to do the early morning runs, and you want to work harder than the opposition. You don't need an alarm clock to wake up; you are excited so your subconscious wakes you up. You are not tempted by junk food, because the picture in your mind of the goal or victory overrides your natural senses. When your dream becomes a magnificent obsession, you go to a whole new level of commitment. You can't stop thinking about it. You go to sleep dreaming about it. You wake up excited about it. Your goals and images of what you want are on your phone, fridge, computer and everywhere. You stop seeing people that hold you back or spurt out poison (negativity). Winning is the only option. This is the power of obsession.

> Winning is the only option. This is the power of obsession.

A magnificent obsession wants to make every moment about the goal and dream so you don't want to do "cheat days" – you skip the cheat days. Champions don't do cheat days. It is hard to do cheat days when you want to win so badly and want your dream so intensely.

SIX

Find Your Superpower

When you find your "super-talent", you find your "superpower".

The problem in life is people abandon or do not use their natural gifts and talents. This is one of the great tragedies and mistakes in our lives. We abandon our dreams as we are often persuaded to be logical and choose the path most choose. Dreamers and history makers choose the path less travelled. These are the ones who set up their own businesses, invent, develop new ideas and pioneer something new. They are highly creative and frequently seen as oddballs, misfits or as unusual. They sacrifice time and effort to climb the highest mountains, win gold medals, receive Nobel prizes and come up with the latest inventions.

All of us have gifts and talents, and the ability to create and innovate. These gifts and abilities may be hidden for years, or remain dormant in the human heart, often not

> The key to winning in life is to recognise and use your unique gifts and talents, and then look for your gift within your gift.

recognised or used. As a coach, I have witnessed some of the biggest singer-songwriters I have developed not know initially they were songwriters. It was only through my encouragement and prompting that they discovered this hidden gift, and then went on to use it and have major hits on the pop charts.

The key to winning in life is to recognise and use your unique gifts and talents, and then look for your gift within your gift. You find your gift within your gift, and then turn it into a super-talent or your superpower.

"If you do what you love, you'll never work a day in your life."

Marc Anthony

Recognising your unique gifts and talents can start very young in life. Look at what subjects in school come easily, and what you are good at. Look at the sports you excel in, any musical gifts and uncommon abilities. This is where greatness starts. Finding your unique gifts and talents can be the game changer for people who are older and unfulfilled in their careers and life. Sometimes we look back at where we excelled, where we were often happiest, and take note of what we were doing back then. Skilled mentors can recognise talent in an individual, and be a great guide and talent developer.

The frustration, for many adults that I speak with is unfulfilled lives, a sense that they are in dead-end jobs. Yes, they are making money, but many are not totally fulfilled. My sense is that many have abandoned their talents, gifts and dreams to pursue the "world" narrative and what we are sold by the media to be success and happiness. Many have so much materialistic "stuff", but they are dead inside, filled with emptiness which may manifest in silent depression and a lack of happiness.

My strong recommendation is that, as adults, we always do deep introspection and ask ourselves, "What do I really want? Am I happy?" Then, if there is something lacking, we should go back and look at our gifts, talents and dreams, and see if there is something we have missed or abandoned along life's journey. Maybe there is a superpower or super-gift that we are not using. Younger people also need to harness and develop their natural gifts and talents, and not abandon them.

The world of USPs in business identifies Unique Selling Propositions for products. As human beings, we have USPs and gifts within gifts. Some may even have "super-gifts".

For instance, as a track athlete, you have sprinters and long distance athletes. Sprinters have fast twitch muscles and are built for speed and power. Long distance runners are built often with slow twitch and are better at the longer endurance races.

In singing, you have singers that have a flare in Rhythm and Blues, where runs and feel are natural. Some are alto (lower voices, rich in tone), mezzo (middle range voices) or sopranos (sing the higher notes with relative ease). You also have different tones and timbres of voices.

As a coach, I always see "the gift within the gift", or what I call the "fast ball" or USP. If we look carefully, every gift can have a greater gift within the gift. For an athlete, it could be an ability for speed; a singer could have a naturally brilliant range or tone.

Your super-gift is that ability or gift that gives you a distinct edge over your opposition.

When you find the gift within the gift, you find the USP or get closer to finding the "gold" or the thing that separates an individual from the masses, from the multitudes. This should then be harnessed and worked on as it gives an individual a natural edge and ability to stand out. Your super-gift is that ability or gift that gives you a distinct edge over your opposition. Many great people discover their gift within a gift, work hard at it, and it becomes a super-gift. Yes, through hard work and dedication, you develop the gift into a super-gift.

Usain Bolt, Michael Jordan and Cristiano Ronaldo were highly gifted athletes who worked day and night to develop their gifts into super-gifts. Michael Jackson, Elvis Presley, Bruno Mars and Prince were all highly gifted entertainers, who developed their craft, and turned their talents into super-talents with hard work and dedication.

I believe one of the reasons many struggle in life is that they fail to recognise or identify their USPs or gifts within gifts. Also, they may not have had mentors that have understood this powerful life-changing principle. Sometimes, families push children into an area that they are not naturally gifted in, as it is what is expected and promoted. Following your natural gifts and USPs is abandoned by many because of these expectations.

The right mentors recognise and see your gifts and potential super-gift; the wrong mentors usually lack energy and passion, are often negative, and can be toxic dream stealers or destroyers. Avoid these at all costs.

I believe the gifts we are given are a divine key to our destinies. We may start in one area, working in our area of gifting, only to find that it leads towards other areas where we find success. Our gift within the gift is like a major river that has tributaries. We start down the river, and the river may divert ... but starting with this divine key is exactly that, it is "the key"!

Some students or adults say to me, "I feel lost, I feel I don't know where I am going with my life." My response is: take stock of your gifts. If necessary, go back to where you excelled in your youth. GIFTS are a divine key to your destiny. If you were previously a sports person, (perhaps with your physician's permission) play sport again. If your gift is singing, sing again; art, paint again. Remember, this may not be your destiny, but it can awaken something inside that becomes like a DOMINO effect that leads you to a happier self, and to unmasking and finding yourself.

As I said in earlier chapters, people are lost and in need of unmasking and finding themselves. Most are living their fake and not their truth. Behind the myriad of masks, who is the real you?

Perhaps true happiness and success lies in unmasking and rebuilding a life you truly love, where you enjoy life and wake up excited. Perhaps you have a potential super-gift you are not using?

Your gift within a gift becomes a massive part of building your brand. This is your strength, your uniqueness – your power. Your uniqueness is your power. Your gift within your gift is your superpower! Sometimes your gift and uniqueness are so great that nobody else has it! It is your main weapon in your trek to winning and having a successful life. Shane Warne found it in spin bowling – a unique style; Muhammad Ali found it in boxing; Michael Jackson found it in pop music and culture.

My story is very similar. At a very young age, from about 3 or 4 years old, I would sing to songs on the radio and sing to people on the trains in the UK where I grew up. We then moved to Singapore when I was aged 6 to 12 years old, before moving to Australia. As I was growing up, I would sing for family events, and later in life, in Australia, my uncle Allan Eaton would always get me to sing at Christmas, and he was the first one to recognise my gift of singing. My dad would also make me sing for the family at family events. At the age of 7, my parents enrolled me in classical piano school, where one of the teachers from the Royal Schools of Music, London, Madam Chew Yew Sen, coached me for several years from her home in Serangoon Gardens, in Singapore. I was invited to perform classical piano concert recitals at

> Your gift within a gift becomes a massive part of building your brand. This is your strength, your uniqueness – your power.

the Hoisington Gallery when I was 8 years old. Vincent Hoisington was an incredible artist and musician and, in fact, was so impressed with my talent and gifting that he gave me a wooden piano with no sound to practise on, and then a few months later a baby grand piano, which stayed in my room for many years beside my bed. I would play and sing for hours. Music and athletics were always a part of my life.

When I was about 7, I realised my athletic gift, and started winning school track events. My music took second place, as I just focused 100 per cent on sport. I was individual track champion at the end of junior school and then high school. My races were the 100 m, 200 m, 400 m and long jump. I also represented the school in basketball, and went on to compete in club competitions in Australia for athletics and basketball. I would train for hours on the track, and hours on the basketball court, with big dreams to represent Australia in either sport.

I put in all the work, but just wasn't quite at the elite level to make the national and international teams. I went on to play and coach basketball for several years.

As I started getting older, music re-emerged in my life. I started taking lessons again, and started winning several singing competitions in Australia, which resulted in me being discovered by industry super manager Ralph Carr and my band Janz becoming world champions.

Yes, I started with many gifts, but my "super-gift" has always been music, singing and writing songs. Discovering this was when everything just exploded. I performed for many years as a professional singer and have sung and toured with some of the greatest singers in the world, including Patti LaBelle, George Benson, Stevie Wonder and many others. I took hundreds of lessons, was relentless in my dedication and practice, outpractised and outworked my peers, and turned my gift into a super-gift to become a world champion and professional singer.

As a coach and mentor to hundreds and thousands of singers for over three decades, I feel coaching is now my "super-gift". God has given me the gift to build champions, stars and a new generation of local and international stars.

> Find and develop your gift into a "super-gift" and focus on it!

Find and develop your gift into a "super-gift" and focus on it! Sometimes you may miss it, like I did for years.

Your super-gift is like your superpower. Find it. Build it. Use it.

Practise Extraordinary When Everyone Is Practising Ordinary

WHEN I LOOK BACK on my life, I wish I had known this truth. I wish I had worked harder, practised more, and used my time more wisely. At 61, I am trying to do catch-up, but youth is a gift, and now I realise the truth in the age-old saying, "youth is wasted on the young". However, not limited by conventional thinking, I am believing in a second wind, and a power finish for the second half of my life.

This is why God gives us mentors and parents who have been down the road you haven't been down yet. They are a light to our path and lamp to our feet. I also now believe that the word of God and motivational/inspirational books can save you years in the wilderness, years of living average and underperforming. The problem is that when we are young, we think we know it all. We are ultimately influenced by culture, radio, media, social media and friends, and we sometimes undervalue our mentors and parents until we are older, and then often regret some of our decisions.

> You cannot practise average and expect extraordinary.

As a result of these poor decisions, we may live a less desirable life, and create our own downfall. Often, if we are honest, it is poor decisions and our own fault that things haven't worked out. Sometimes we can blame others, but most often it is our own fault. This is the case with my life.

You cannot practise average and expect extraordinary.

Always watch what the average is doing, and do more. Train more. Study more. Discipline yourself more. The key is more.

Practising extraordinary is the gaining of wisdom, realising the incredible value of mentors, making great mentors part of your life, becoming a student of success by reading success story books, watching success videos, surrounding yourself with people who inspire you even if it's one or two. It is being highly disciplined, eliminating compromise and cheat days, valuing time and being selfish with where you spend it. Learning to prioritise your life and say "no". No to the food that hurts you, no to people who drain you and pull you down, no to self-destructive habits, and, most of all, no to blaming the world when things don't work out. Take ownership. This is practising extraordinary.

It takes effort and sacrifice to go against the tide – to think differently, act differently and build a life that is different to the norm. Practising extraordinary takes sacrifice, commitment, discipline and willpower.

When you embark on a fitness regime, eating protocol or even start to dream big, the greatest force that will come up against you is other people's opinions. It may start at home, at school, at the workplace, or among friends. It comes in the form of negative words or subtle comments that artfully or overtly have the underlying motive of discouragement.

We have all been programmed as "agents of conformity". As soon as we see someone coming out of what is considered normal, we start becoming the "conformity police". Our goal is to bring people back to what looks like average or below average. Success rattles many. Actions that are extraordinary become the enemy, and society enlists the conformity police to step into action.

When you start losing weight, people have an opinion; when you decide to open a business or start a new venture, people have an opinion. Most bow down to peer group pressure, and the goals set at New Year's Eve are abandoned, and most join the masses in the pursuit of average. Most cheat on diets and fail. Most start a dream or venture and quit because it becomes too hard, and friends are just playing it safe or average.

You often hear the words "be normal". This is often the phrase used to pull down extraordinary actions. Some will say, "You look too thin," if you start dieting, or "You look good," when you are nowhere near your goal. Some will tell you to relax, take it easy and to have a cheat moment or day.

The problem with a cheat day, or compromise, is you risk it becoming a habit. It is amazing how a break in discipline or commitment to a goal can lead to years of failure at a goal. Most people start a diet routine, gym or another endeavour, then decide one day to cheat or have a break. This is the number one reason, years later, that nothing has been achieved, and the main reason people fail at a goal or goals. Compromise is the killer of dreams and goals. Cheat days kill dreams and champions. This is why there is only one Cristiano Ronaldo and it is hard to be a champion.

People then usually blame life or bad circumstances for their lack of success. The reason people fail is they sometimes let bad habits kill their potential destinies. They blame everyone but themselves.

This is why the quest for greatness and the extraordinary can be a lonely road as you carefully choose and navigate through choices, where you go and who you associate with. You also realise that most of us consciously, or subconsciously, have been programmed and recruited as "conformity agents" to quash dreamers and drag people back to normal.

This is why encouragement is so incredibly rare. Sadly, when students do well in singing and emerge as potential stars, they often don't get a lot of likes on social media. In fact, the abuse and negativity so many stars receive is heartbreaking. People would much rather be critical and negative, rather than encourage, praise and uplift. Encouragement and praise is as rare as gold. There are very few people-builders and many more dream-crushers. Just look at the comments, or lack of comments, on social media. Wow.

> The reason people fail is they sometimes let bad habits kill their potential destinies. They blame everyone but themselves.

Criticism and negativity is a form of bringing people back to normal and conformity. Sadly, this is in every endeavour and field.

Surround yourself with encouragers and people who propel you up.

As mentioned earlier, the people who are the least successful in a field often make themselves authorities in areas that they know nothing about. This can be friends, family members, associates and even strangers.

Surround yourself with encouragers and people who propel you up. If they have a track record of success, they will then constructively and positively show you where to improve. The most destructive force in the world is negativity and negative words spoken over you. The most powerful force in the world is positivity and mentors who see the greatness in you, encourage you and propel you to awaken the giant in you.

The most influential teacher I had at school was Kay Coghlan, during my time at Thornbury High School in Melbourne. Up until this point, I had some very good teachers, but Mrs Coghlan made the classroom come alive. She was in a different league. She made me feel important, corrected me often, but always told me I had a gift for English literature and writing, and that I could get top marks for my VCE creative subjects. And, as she predicted, I got an A for English literature!

Midway through my final year, Mrs Coghlan called my mother in for a meeting and recommended that I focus on the arts and my creative gifts, as this was where I was strong. She suggested that I drop Chemistry, so that I had one less subject and could concentrate on my strengths and really excel. This was a critical moment and a turning point in my life, as I dropped Chemistry, which I was struggling in, and put all of my efforts for the rest of the year in my creative subjects. Thanks to Mrs Coghlan, I finished the year doing so well.

Mrs Coghlan also taught me a very powerful life lesson, that everyone has their own special gifts and talents, and to focus on where you're gifted and make these gifts stronger. Mrs Coghlan changed my life, and as I became a coach to thousands myself, her principles have contributed to the many stars I have coached from the ground up. I will never forget her excitement, her smile and her eyes that communicated love and belief in me.

One "Mrs Coghlan" in your life can change the trajectory of your life, and like a powerful force, change the trajectory of generations through you. Mrs Coghlan is a generational changer!

As a coach, when students come in, I don't just want to teach singing, I want to teach them the art of winning. I see my work as generational. I want it to be the highlight of their week. I want to transform them and instil self-belief in them. It is not just brilliant singing – I want them all to develop the mindset and habits of champions. I want to awaken the giant in each one of my students. I want to awaken giants ... When people ask me what I do as a career, I say "I awaken giants".

You can have the greatest talent in the world, but if you don't have the mindset and work ethic of champions, you won't make it. This is why, in my work on building champions, I spend just as much time working on the inner stuff as I do on the voice. The world is full of "could have beens" and "should have beens" in all arenas of life who were just uneducated in the area of mindset, success acumen and just never put in the hard work.

Finally, I believe there should be a subject in every school in the world called "the mindset and work ethic of champions" taught from junior to high school levels.

Become a people-builder

The mark of a true leader is someone who understands that everyone has their own road to travel and is never intimidated by or jealous of someone else's success.

The highest, most noble path in life is to help someone else achieve their dreams and goals.

The power of saying "no"

There is great power in learning to say "no".

"No" brings the choices back to you, and it helps you focus on where you want to invest your time and energy. It is a powerful word that champions are comfortable saying.

In the area of goals and dreams, where you spend your time and energy will determine whether you succeed or not. In the area of people you associate with, this is critical too. Keep away from people who pull you away from your goals and dreams through negativity or poor lifestyle choices.

Focus on your goals and targets, and invest your time and energy on the goals most important to you. Do not veer away, or allocate time and energy to projects that do not help you achieve your goals.

Be a miser with your time. This is your most precious resource.

> "No" brings the choices back to you, and it helps you focus on where you want to invest your time and energy.

Every day do something positive that moves you closer to your goals and dreams. We sometimes feel obligated to say "yes" to everything, as we are trained to be people-pleasers and don't want to let anyone down. Compromise is also everyone's norm, so we quite easily have cheat days or move away from goals, or don't even have goals.

Champions are comfortable saying "no" as they understand it is like a powerful rudder that will steer them to victory in life. A life of winning. "No" then becomes a power word, one of your most valuable resources to you winning.

NO!

EIGHT

Invest in Great Mentors

YOU CANNOT PUT A value or price on a great mentor and coach. They push you, inspire you, and the great ones help draw out the best part of you and give you keys to victory in your chosen endeavour. Coaches see your blind spots, they see what you don't see and work on you becoming better. The best coaches have a track record of wins and are the best in their fields.

Investing in world class coaches and trainers can save you time, money and wasted years.

Major reasons so many people fail to achieve greatness are:

1. They fail to see the value of investment in great coaches.
2. They don't look for the best.
3. They are not willing to travel or sacrifice to get to the best.

This applies in any field – financial planners, business coaches, gym trainers, singing coaches, athletic coaches, managers, producers, record labels ... look for their track record. Always recruit the best, no matter the cost.

There is nothing more expensive than unfulfilled dreams, unused talent and a life of mediocrity, because you failed to invest in great mentors and coaches. To be the best, train with the best.

> Investing in world class coaches and trainers can save you time, money and wasted years.

My dad was a great mentor in my early formative years. At 8 years old, I was a great sprinter, so he would encourage me to get up at 5 am to train. He would always rebuke me for my limited thinking and lack of self-belief. He would always tell me to think big. He also pushed me academically to excel.

For years I thought he was cruel and harsh, but God gave me the dad I needed. Truly an incredible dad who instilled in my heart, and being, the keys to victory.

Dad had a fantastic personal brand, would always dress like a superstar, pick interesting colours, and when he walked into a room, everyone would stop and look. Dad was also a brilliant artist and was a creative director for George Patterson Advertising Asia/Pacific.

He lived in the lane of uniqueness, personal brand, strong self-belief and faith. I remember one story clearly. As a young boy, I was at an inter-school athletics competition, and I was about to race in the final of the 400 m sprint. I told my dad that there was no way I could beat a particular boy from another school, and my dad replied that not only would I win the race, but that I would break the all-time record as well. He told me that I had already won the race, and that I should now focus on breaking the record. He said that victory is in the mind, then tactically told me how to run the race.

I won the race by 40 metres, and broke the state record that year. That is the power of great mentors and coaches, and I am so grateful for my dad, whom I sadly lost quite early in life.

Later in life, in my health journey, I have recruited my personal gym coach who is a world champion herself and trains elite bodybuilders, Areti Anagnostellis from Tabban Gym. As a singer, I have trained with the best coaches, but superstar Patti LaBelle really changed everything for me. I am grateful for all of the mentors and coaches in my life.

My inspirational close friend, John Gian, has also changed my life and impacted my life greatly. He lives and breathes motivation and inspiration. At the critical points in my life, he was there. He guided me to a wholefood, plant-based diet, when my wife, Lynn, and I were getting more overweight and sick; he taught me some powerful principles that helped me build Jaanz International Singing Academy; his long talks and guidance in my youth shaped the leader I am today.

If I have missed you, I am sorry, but thank you to all of my mentors and coaches who have shaped me over the years.

NINE

Goals Are Your Gold

SETTING GOALS, AND REVIEWING them constantly, is the most important habit to develop.

Written goals give you a target and something to aim at.

Look at your goals daily. Visualise achieving them. Display them on a dream board or on your phone.

The key is to visualise yourself achieving your goals. See it in your mind on replay.

Goals give you the "power of the reset".

The power of the reset states "you can change your life at any point of time using the power of goals, intense and constant visualisation and then daily acting on these goals".

We need to do "something daily" – yes, daily – to action these goals. So, for instance, if you want to lose weight, you are consistent with your diet and training.

As a singer, you practise your scales daily, write songs, go to weekly lessons etc.

Why people fail to achieve their dreams starts here:

1. They never write down goals.
2. They never action goals.
3. They are believers in the cheat day myth.

This is a simple formula to win. Most will sadly not.

You also activate the power of the reset with affirmations. Say it like it has already happened. "I have greatness in me, I am fearfully and wonderfully made ..." etc.

The best affirmation is the one you personalise and make to suit you like it's already happened. Visualise it too.

Review your goals, visualise your goals and say your personal affirmations.

Words have power and when you direct them to your goals in a positive way it gives your goals a life and power.

Listen to the most successful people in the world talk – Muhammad Ali, Floyd Mayweather, Cristiano Ronaldo and so many others.

They often declare victory even before the competition begins.

They are masters at the art of goal setting and bringing life to their goals with action, discipline and the power of words.

Resilience

Resilience is a word that few know, and even fewer apply. This is the reason the richest place in the world is the cemetery. The cemetery is full of people buried with talents, dreams and potential unused. This is mainly because many simply gave up on their dreams and abandoned their gifts and talents after receiving rejection, disappointment or discouragement.

They gave up after one or two failures, or after one or two or more knock-backs.

Champions have learnt to get up from the hits of life. They understand that they need to learn the art of resilience, or bouncing back from defeat. Getting up often from the canvas of life. Like a boxer, we need to take the hits, but keep getting up and staying the course.

> Like a boxer, we need to take the hits, but keep getting up and staying the course.

The world is full of rejects who kept going, kept fighting and became champions.

Let the scars and hurts of defeat make you a star in life and the pursuit of your dreams.

Tenacity

To be tenacious means to hold on, hold on with every ounce of strength.

> Let the scars and hurts of defeat make you a star in life and the pursuit of your dreams.

This is also a word that few know, and fewer practise.

Through tears, heartbreak and disappointment, you hold on to your dream then action it by consistently doing the daily things needed to win. No compromise. No days off. No cheat days.

Resilience and tenacity become the twin attributes that champions use to propel them to victory. Watch the champions; they are a success book in real time. All you need to know about winning is written in their lives and life stories.

TEN

Victory starts with the Mouth

THERE IS A POWER when we realise that victory starts with the mouth. There is a supernatural power, and natural power, that comes into play when we learn the power of "fasting" and eliminating certain foods from our diet. We also learn that what we say matters, and spoken words have incredible creative power!

It truly sets off a catalyst to victory in nearly every area of our lives. When we can conquer what we put in our mouths, we actually win the greater battles, our health improves dramatically, we learn self-discipline and control, we start achieving other goals, our self- esteem improves, we get greater mental clarity, and we start feeling invincible.

When you can say "no" and consciously choose what goes into your mouth, you build the inner self or the inner man/woman. You see, one of the strongest senses in the human body is to enjoy food, satisfy our tastebuds and satiate our cravings, and eat whatever we desire.

When we can discipline and conquer this desire, and say "no", it sets off a catalyst to an inner strength, of which many of us are unaware.

Jesus fasted. Gandhi fasted. Saint Daniel in the Bible fasted. Many of the Indian gurus fast and pray. Fasting builds an inner strength. When we discipline what goes in our mouths, it is a form of fasting, as we say "no" to certain foods. This has many natural benefits, but also spiritual benefits as we build the inner spirit to conquer the outer.

In fact, being a vegan is a lifestyle similar to Saint Daniel's fast. Saint Daniel was offered all of the rich food of the king, but rejected it for a vegan diet, and he was healthier and stronger compared to those eating the king's diet of foods similar to today's Western world foods.

When my wife and I go out to restaurants, we have very limited choices, as we are vegan but also don't consume oil with our foods. Because of this, we always eat before going out with friends or family for a meal, and usually opt for a salad or fruit salad. We also look for vegan-friendly restaurants that can prepare the meals without oil.

This takes planning, commitment, sacrifice and discipline.

Building the inner spirit is the key to every outward victory.

As mentioned earlier, "words matter" and what comes out of our mouth is like a rudder that can steer us to victory or defeat in life. Often when we are callous with our words, these can have tragic consequences. We give our competitors the advantage when we sabotage victory with one or two words of submission or defeat.

> Building the inner spirit is the key to every outward victory.

It is almost like there is a power in optimism and positivity we can never underestimate. The most successful students I have ever coached have clear goals and are very careful what they say. We need to guard our mouths more and sometimes we sabotage our destinies by not taking heed of our "off the cuff" words of negativity, which sadly may seal our fate or abort our dreams.

ELEVEN

Never Quit

WHEN THE "WORD" BECOMES louder than the voice of our critics, quitting is not an option.

As mentioned earlier, whether it's your subconscious, instinct, or gut feeling, often the inner voice, or "the word", is a guide from a higher, deeper source. The word in your heart or gut has to swallow up and become larger than any setback or any negativity from others. My belief is this inner voice is a guide to your destiny and your life's purpose.

So many music stars, CEOs, owners of businesses, athletes etc. have emerged to win after being highly discouraged at the beginning of their journey. The key is to hold on to your dream, hold on to the word in your heart, or even a word of destiny spoken over you, from someone you value, or even your mentor.

There was a very tough point in my music career where one of the A and R representatives from one of the major record labels came to see my band Janz and me perform. After the show he pulled me aside and he said to me, "You will never make it – you are black, Indian, and perhaps you should choose another career. You will never make it in music."

The "word" in my heart simply dismissed his comments, although racist and hurtful. A few weeks later we beat 22,000 bands from around the world in the World Yamaha Competition and a senior member from his label signed me. I remember going into the label's boardroom and seeing this A and R person fuming, his face virtually red with anger and embarrassment. Three decades later I am here writing this book, having coached so many stars, champions and leaders not just in the field of singing but also in life.

If I had listened to his damaging, negative words there would be no Janz, David Jaanz and the legacy of champions God has used me to inspire, love and encourage.

The most beautiful thing in life is a mentor who speaks life, creates a vision that we cannot see at the time, points to incredible possibilities in us, the unlimited potential in us, yet reminds us of the work and sacrifice required to achieve the dream. I have been blessed to have some amazing mentors who did just this.

I am particularly blessed to have the most supportive wife, Lynn Jaanz, who sees the best in me, pushes me to be better, is loving and kind to me even through my frequent stubbornness and my misguided choices. I am blessed to have found the love of my life in her and every day with Lynn is a piece of heaven. She too is a highly successful master singing coach and international artist who is recognised globally for her incredible artwork. She is more than a wife – she is a powerful mentor and every day she encourages me to be the best version of myself. (www.lynnjaanzartgallery.com)

Write down your dream and hold on to it with every bit of your heart. Chase it daily and remember, you only have one life so live a happy life, love extravagantly and most of all believe in yourself.

Don't let people project their limitations on you. What the mind can conceive and believe, the mind can achieve.

Let the word grow daily larger than the opinion of the doubters.

Go for gold. Go for the win!

TWELVE

Put God First

Everyone has a moment where everything can suddenly change. I have told you many of these moments throughout this book, but the whole trajectory of my life took a dramatic turn when I committed my life to Jesus Christ in 1996.

To this point I didn't believe in much. I was riddled with severe depression, anxiety and unhappiness. I was unfulfilled and had everything a man could want materially but was poor in happiness.

In fact, to be very honest, I was suicidal for several years.

As I opened my heart to the Holy Spirit and my relationship with Christ, he started working on me, transforming me over time. He teaches me and changes me.

Over time, my depression left, and my life went from victory to victory.

Today I am free of depression. Now I enjoy a peace every day that I cannot explain.

I am by no means a perfect man, but I am always a work in progress. I have a contentment and fulfilment that I cannot explain.

I immersed myself for years in the study of scripture and prayer. Even though as a believer the storms and struggles kept coming in my life, I kept the faith.

I never stopped believing. I often cried for days sometimes, but I got up and kept going.

Like Elvis Presley, Whitney Houston, Aretha Franklin, Billy Graham and so many others that have walked the path of faith and found the light, in our imperfections, our faith and hope is in a creator who walks with us in this life.

He understands our human struggles and frailties and is a creator who loves us.

My faith in Christ and the Holy Spirit was the beginning of victory after victory.

*"For God so loved the world that
he gave his only begotten son that
whoever believes in him should not
perish but have eternal life."*

John 3:16

I believe each one of you has the capability to become a champion. This is not a once-read type of book. I pray that, just like the Bible, this is a book you can come back to, to remind you of the champion you can be if you decide to put the hard work in.

Sending love to all of you who have read my book and enjoyed it. May you enjoy a life filled with every blessing, success and joy abundantly.

My final word – put God first.

*"Seek the kingdom of God first
and his righteousness and all
things will be added to you."*

Matthew 6:33

With love,
David